JACQUES PERRIN - GALATÉE FILMS PRESENTS

WINGED MIGRATION

THE JUNIOR EDITION

BY **STÉPHANE DURAND** AND **GUILLAUME POYET**

seuil chronicle

Contents

More than 20,000 years ago, when prehistoric people were still painting on cave walls, enormous glaciers crept down over Europe, Asia, and North America. Every place began to look like Siberia. To feed themselves, our ancestors went on long risky hunts in pursuit of herds of reindeer, woolly rhinoceros, and mammoth. Advancing ice kept pushing the northern frontier of plant and animal life farther south.

Then gradually, as the centuries went by, temperatures rose again and the grip of the glaciers loosened. So slowly that no one even noticed, the snow line retreated back into the high mountains in the north, leaving behind fields of stones soon covered by mosses and lichens. These pioneer plants led the way for the first grasses and trees, in which birds from milder climates would soon perch.

Birds, too, ventured farther north. Used to mild temperatures, they encountered a whole new problem there: winter. They learned that each year, cold descends for several months. Plants dry up, insects disappear, snow covers entire regions. Life seems to hold its breath. And so, to find food and shelter, birds had to go back south. But as soon as winter began to wane, they started flocking north again. This is how today's migration routes originated.

At the very beginning of the glaciers' retreat, birds' summer habitats weren't very large, nor were they all that far from their winter homes. Their migrations thus did not take very long. But little by little, the distances grew—today, birds sometimes have to travel several thousand miles to return to their winter habitats!

Not all birds migrate. Many species have adapted to winter by exploiting the few food resources available during winter months: buds, seeds, and fruit remaining on trees, or insects hidden in the recesses of bark. But these sedentary birds are the minority. When fall arrives, most birds living in temperate and northern climates anticipate the arrival of the cold and hurriedly build up the reserves of body fat they need for the journey south. Because they don't know what food they will find along the way, some as much as double their weight.

Today, billions of birds worldwide migrate every year, following thousands of different routes over every continent. Rain, fog, sandstorms, vast oceans, towering mountains, scorching deserts, glacial ice fields, power cables, hunters, oil slicks, and pollution all take their toll on the birds. Small-sized species such as swallows can lose almost half of their population in less than a year.

But whether they fly solo or in flocks, by day or night, whether they instinctively know their route or learn it by following their parents, migratory birds all have an extraordinary sense of direction. They can launch into long-distance journeys knowing they will find their wintering grounds with the utmost precision. Some even return to the very nest where they were born. They do this by using maps engraved in their memories. Three-dimensional, and incorporating the sun or stars as a guide, these memory maps tell the birds about prevailing winds, magnetic fields, and sometimes even smells.

Each of the tales you are about to read illustrates the extraordinary capacity of birds to adapt to different environments. Some travel from the North Pole to the South Pole, others fly over the world's highest mountains, still others no longer fly but swim. Birds have found solutions to every environmental obstacle and constraint—a humbling lesson for us self-proclaimed masters of this world.

Knights of the Skies
White Storks

EUROPE

ASIA

AFRICA

BREEDING

WINTERING

Imagine Constantinople in the year 1204: Crusaders laying siege to the citadel are battling the Byzantines. Fearsome warriors are locked in hand-to-hand combat. The clashing of swords and cries of pain rise from the city. Clouds of arrows fall from the sky in deadly showers. Horses, eyes bulging with fright, try as best they can to pick their way through this mass of human fury. When the sun sets on the carnage, the blood-red light of dusk, like a death shroud, cloaks the knights lying where they died. As night falls, a host of tiny white dots appears and lands. A curtain of darkness descends over the scene, smothering the sobs of pain and grief.

Fast forward to modern Constantinople, now called Istanbul. It is September. The sun rises like a ball of fire. From the glinting minarets of the city's many mosques, muezzins are calling the faithful to prayer. As the mosques' mosaics glitter in the growing, golden light, what appears all these centuries later but the same host of white dots, a silent spiral in the sky. Standing in a square, people from around the world lower their binoculars and jump for joy. "Look! White storks. Thousands of them." French, English, Spanish, American, Japanese, and African bird-watchers all cheer, their eyes never leaving the sky.

The storks have already flown so far, some from Germany and Poland, others from Hungary. There is a legend that in the spring they deposit their babies in chimneys when they return from their long journey. But these storks still have a long way to go before their journey's over. They're flying south to join the elephants and the giraffes in the heart of Africa.

On their way there, the storks fly over a symbolic city, Jerusalem, the hallowed place where the Koran and the Bible mingle and where, alas, many bloody battles have also been fought. When they finally reach the savannas south of the Sahara, where plagues of crickets are devouring every last blade of grass, these knights-errant come to the aid of humans by snapping up the voracious insects with their long beaks.

Height: 43 inches
Weight: 5–10 pounds
Wingspan: 68–76 inches
Flight speed: 22–31 mph

During the breeding season, stork couples greet each other by repeatedly snapping their beaks and making wheezing noises.
Their nests can weigh several hundred pounds (up to a ton), since they are generally reused and reinforced with more branches and twigs every year.
To take flight and cover long distances, gliding birds such as storks ride the thermals (rising columns of hot air) created either by the sun heating the ground or by changes in terrain. By gliding without beating their wings, they can save up to ninety percent of their energy! Unfortunately, these favorable weather conditions do not exist at sea.
The oldest-known stork lived to be 33 years old.

In the shadows, an old man looks on in silence and smiles faintly. He knows, from the writings of his ancestors, that these are no ordinary migratory birds. They are the knights of the sky. He knows that during that battle in 1204 the storks landed here, then took to the air again with the souls of the fallen soldiers. The red of their beak and legs reminds us of the blood those men shed, while the white of their bodies is a symbol of peace. The old man knows that, unlike other birds, they do not fly over the seas but prefer to fly over land, in order to be seen by the greatest number of people, to awaken a glimmer of goodness in everyone who beholds them.

Knights of the sky, you are above all frontiers and battles, above religion. Just your simple white line through the sky is enough to open the doors of the heart!

Guacamayos
Blue-and-Gold Macaws

AMAZONIA

SOUTH AMERICA

PRESENT YEAR-ROUND

Have you ever woken up as the first rays of sun are just beginning to warm the morning air, and felt a calm harmony deep within you? Owls and bats vanish from the sky, making way for the creatures of the day. And yet there is a land, deep in the heart of the Amazon forest, where dawn is accompanied by sobs said to come from a river.

Amazonia, goddess with green eyes! Vast forest stretching as far as human eyes can see, where the jaguar reigns supreme. Silently it creeps up on its prey. As though suddenly aware of the threat, the deer shivers. It scans the surrounding undergrowth, staring into every patch of shadow. An eerie silence falls. When, after several seconds, nothing happens, the deer's fright begins to fade. Reassured, it resumes grazing, and never sees the fleeting silhouette that leaps from the undergrowth. High in the forest's cathedral-like vaults, before taking flight, two long-tailed birds hear a short plaintive cry in the dense foliage below.

A glimmer of light has appeared in the east. The high humidity that steeps the forest is beginning to evaporate, forming little clouds that cling to the treetops. The river winding through the waking forest gleams like a great golden snake. Suddenly an incredible cacophony of shrieks rises from the water. Just as it does every day, the river is weeping, screaming. This is one of the Forest Mother's many secrets, the secret of the *guacamayos*. The native peoples call these blue-and-gold macaws "cries of the river." Magnificent birds with powerful beaks and blue-and-yellow plumage the color both of the sky and the golden sun, guacamayos have the ability to imitate everything they hear. It is they who fly to the

Height: 33 inches
Weight: 34–38 ounces
Wingspan: 28–31 inches
Flight speed: 22–43 mph

▶ The blue-and-gold macaw uses its hooked beak like a third foot to climb and cling to trees. Its powerful feet and beak are also very useful for feeding: a macaw will grip fruit with its claws and then carefully break it open with its beak to extract the flesh and seeds.

▶ Blue-and-gold macaws congregate on cliffs along riverbanks to eat the clay-rich soil. The clay they ingest lines their stomach, protecting them from the acidic and sometimes poisonous fruits they eat.

▶ Blue-and-gold macaws can live up to 80 years.

▶ To make its nest, it digs a three- to six-foot hole in a palm tree with its beak.

outermost limits of the green kingdom and perch in the tree canopy to watch and listen. Then they return to announce all the news to the inhabitants of the forest.

At dawn, they gather on treetops along the riverbanks. They deliver the most important news, news that unfortunately, for a long time now, has always been bad. At their daily riverside assemblies, there has long been only one subject of conversation. The people of the forest are worried, because the guacamayos are weeping to warn other forest dwellers of terrible danger. They have seen big, black smoke-belching animals pluck up scores of trees, tie them in bundles, and throw them into the nearest river. There, at the green kingdom's fringes, towering walls of flame are devouring the forest. Desperately, the creatures that live there flee for their lives. Some of the frantic animals stop in their tracks and collapse, struck dead by steely eyes that spit deadly venom after a short thunderclap.

In many places around the world, dawn is peaceful, serene, and harmonious, but in the Amazon rain forest, the guacamayos continue to scream. Great is the distress of the green Amazon goddess. Perhaps one day, when the flames cease, the birds will sing a melodious song of hope instead. And the dawn's golden rays will caress the goddess's long green hair. Perhaps one day she will wake up in peace and the river will flow without tears.

NORTH AMERICA
GREENLAND
ICELAND
EUROPE
ATLANTIC OCEAN

■ BREEDING
☐ WINTERING

Njord's People

Atlantic Puffins

Thick fog has drifted down from the fjords and swirls slowly over the ocean. Every form appears ghostlike. A faint, diffuse light gathers imperceptibly. A dark shape like a rearing serpent traces a silent wake through the merging sea and fog. Deep voices ring out— Vikings on board a sculpted longship.

The chief calmly peers into the dense fog, looking out for the slightest sign of danger or the faintest call from the Beyond. "Is Njord, god of the winds and the sea, with us this time?" he asks himself, and wonders if the fog is a warning to turn back. The crew left Scandinavia several weeks ago. By now they are cold and their faces are etched with fatigue. Their chief does not want his men to see the doubt overcoming him, so he stays perfectly erect, like the prow of his ship, patiently listening, watching. The crew members have their weapons at the ready, for Vikings are not afraid of death. If they die valiantly, they believe they will enter Valhalla, the kingdom of the gods. But the enemy facing them now is fluid, and no matter how razor sharp their swords, they would slice through nothing. Has Njord forsaken them, delivered them into the hands of the demons of the unknown universe?

Suddenly ten black-and-white, short-winged little creatures, their beaks full of fish, leap out of the sea to starboard and speed off into the fog together. More splashing is heard on the port side, and seven more take off out of the water. "Fisher birds who have mastered the worlds of both sea and air! Could this magic be Njord's doing?" The chief immediately orders his oarsmen to follow these strange creatures. As they journey on, the fog lifts and they encounter more and more of these tiny beings, which can swim under the sea and then take flight.

"Land ahoy!" someone shouts from the stern of the ship. The chief spots cliffs looming ahead in the fog. Perched on their steep grassy slopes are the short-winged creatures. Like primitive cave dwellers, they have homes burrowed in the earth. The Viking chief smiles to himself, and inwardly thanks "Njord's people" for having shown him the way. There will be no need to draw swords; for him this land will always be synonymous with peace.

The year was 874, and Norwegian Viking Ingolfur Arnarson and his crew had just discovered Iceland. If you read about this in history books today, you won't find the role of Njord's people ever mentioned. But some say that the Viking chief's last wish was to be buried next to the birds, for they were the only creatures ever to have given him a peaceful welcome.

Njord's people—what we call Atlantic puffins—still inhabit Iceland today. From their cliff-top homes, they continue to watch ships cross the vast ocean.

Height: 12 inches
Weight: 18 ounces
Wingspan: 18–25 inches
Flight speed: 37–50 mph

▸ Puffins nest in colonies on grassy slopes and cliffs. Colonies can comprise hundreds of thousands of birds. They nest in three- to six-foot-deep burrows, which they hollow out with their beaks and claws. A single egg is laid inside. The chick leaves the nest at around forty days old, usually at night to avoid predators such as falcons and gulls.

▸ In flight, puffins beat their wings up to 300 or 400 times per minute!

▸ A puffin's tongue has a series of backward-slanting spines, which enable it to grip several fish in its beak at once. The red beak turns gray during winter, until the following mating season.

▸ The Atlantic puffin is sometimes called the "sea clown" or "sea parrot."

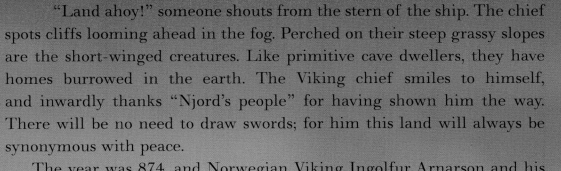

Dancers of the Taiga
Common Cranes

BREEDING

WINTERING

ASIA

EUROPE

AFRICA

"My grandfather's grandfather spent the winter here. It's a small area in Spain whose oak-dotted savannas look just like those in Africa. We have been making this journey for centuries, ever since cranes can remember.

"We stayed here for three tranquil months, pecking at acorns in the southern sun. We sleep standing up in the marsh, hidden among the reeds. For the past few days, we have felt spring coming: the temperature is getting milder, the days longer. The first cranes on their way home from Africa are squawking as they tidy up their nests. Great bustards gather in the fields to rehearse their ecstatic displays. Each day we get more and more excited, seeing who can jump the highest or run the fastest in any direction, twirling around and shouting at the tops of our voices. When I say 'us,' I mean the adults. They're the ones who are getting the most agitated. I'm too young still, only two years old! My head hasn't turned black and white yet, and I don't have a little red cap over my eyes like my parents do.

"This morning, a flight of cranes landed among us, making long guttural calls that rolled on the air. They were coming from a little farther south—some had even spent the winter in Morocco. Their arrival set off a joyous din—the signal for us to leave. So, one after the other, we took flight and in large Vs or long lines, flying in Indian file, we set off on our first, 600-mile nonstop flight. Each of us takes a turn flying in front to set the pace—it's the most tiring position!

"I made my first journey one fall with my parents, who knew every inch of the way. We flew over the whole of Europe to get to Spain. This is my third migration without my parents. I prefer now to travel with cranes my age. Now it's our job to guide the younger ones who have just left their parents.

16

"I'll have no trouble finding the taiga, the conifer forest, in Sweden, where I was born. I'll recognize every mountain, valley, and river on our 2,000-mile journey. I've learned how to navigate by the sun, and I know the map of the stars by heart. All I worry about is bad weather—thick clouds that might hide the sun and stars, or a strong head wind that could ground us for days or even weeks. Worst of all is when we unexpectedly hit bad weather while we're flying. It's like suddenly being blindfolded—all you can do is follow your lucky star.

"This is why, when the weather permits, we fly as fast and far as possible. It's possible to do the journey in only a few days, but there are always three or four long stopovers on the way, to rest and stock up on food. If all goes well, we'll be back in Scandinavia around a month after we left Spain.

"What I like doing best in Scandinavia is exploring the marshes and peat bogs where delicate cotton grass waves in the breeze and sundews, a type of carnivorous plant, exude a gluey dew. All around, as far as the eyes can see, there are dark taigas whose trees, covered with long beards of gray lichen, look like they're 1,000 years old. Underneath them are enormous lumps of granite and worm-eaten trunks covered with a thick carpet of moss that keeps out unwanted visitors. They say goblins and trolls live in the taiga. But still, it's where couples pair up to reproduce. Well, when I say 'us,' I really mean the adults. I'm still too young. Maybe next year …"

Crane couples stay together for life and are extremely secretive during the breeding season. Both parents sit on their two eggs for about thirty days. The precocious chicks can run, swim, and hide when in danger. Each parent rears, protects, and feeds one of the two chicks, which will be able to fly at nine to ten weeks old. During this period, the parents lose all their feathers to grow new ones, and so are incapable of flying for about five weeks. This complete molt happens every two to four years.

Cranes eats everything: roots, tubers, leaves, fruit and seeds, and, in summer, insects, snails, earthworms, frogs, lizards, and even small rodents.

Height: 43 inches
Weight: 9–13 pounds
Wingspan: 7–8 feet
Flight speed: 19–50 mph

Greenland
Atlantic Ocean
Antarctica

Sea Swallows
Arctic Terns

Breeding

Wintering

Sitting on a rock, smoking his pipe, an old man gazes over the undulating ocean at the endless horizon stretching before him. The sea has been his whole life; he could not live without it. As he sits there, lost in his memories, his eyes fill with salty tears. When he was young, lively as a mackerel, thirsty for adventures, he went to sea as a cabin boy on a boat fishing for cod in the great North Sea.

"Let the waves carry me far from my village, let the sea roll its great wet drum!" he declared.

His captain was proud of him. The lot of a cabin boy wasn't easy: cleaning and polishing, and hauling the nets out of the freezing sea with your bare hands. Your skin was endlessly being grazed by fish fins and eaten into by salt. There was no time for daydreaming. But the sheer joy of being at sea canceled out these daily hardships.

After a heavy storm, his captain gave the order to drop anchor in one of those famous Nordic fjords to repair the damage. Not far from a lagoon at the foot of a glacier, he set eyes on a wonderful sight: a bird colony on the Arctic tundra. They were genuine sea swallows—white birds with slender wings perfect for flying long distances and navigating violent winds, plus indented tails with frayed edges. As he watched parents bringing fish back to their young, and males offering mates their catch, he saw that love existed there, too, far from the world of human beings.

Amid this happiness in the shining sun, he noticed a young orphan chick. He decided to feed it and take care of it, and soon it grew into a fine-looking bird. It began to fly, venturing out over the lagoon at the foot of the glacier and learning to dive for fish. The young tern would perch on the icebergs with other birds its age. The cabin boy smiled: thanks to him the bird had been able to take flight and discover its—and his—true element, the sea! And as soon as he appeared on the banks of the lagoon, the bird would come back to greet him.

As a memento of their bond—that of two creatures of the sea—he placed a brass band around one of the bird's legs. The weather began to change; the

Height: 15 inches
Weight: 4 pounds
Wingspan: 29–33 inches
Flight speed: 25 mph

▶ The arctic tern is the very emblem of migration since every year it covers up to 12,500 miles on its journey from the North Pole, where it breeds, to its fishing grounds around the South Pole, where it winters. Because its yearly migration takes it from the boreal to the austral summers, it is the bird that enjoys the most daylight during its lifetime.

▶ To attract females and choose a partner, the male flies with a small fish in its beak, which he offers to the female following him.

▶ The nest can be a bed of dried grass or merely a hollow made in dry, stony ground. The female usually lays two eggs, whose incubation takes twenty to twenty-four days. After a few days, the young chicks leave the nest to better protect themselves from predators. They begin to fly at around three weeks old.

air grew colder and it sometimes snowed. The sea swallows made their farewell flight around the lagoon: around they went in a wide circle, calling to the other birds, and then suddenly they were off, heading due south over the sea.

What invisible force suddenly took hold of their slender bodies and drove them away across the ocean, toward the unknown? He saw so much of himself in them.

Years went by. He had become a fully fledged seaman with a good many voyages under his belt. He was down in the southern seas on a whaler, on the other side of world from his village on the North Sea coast. A raging storm had come upon them, and as the ship pitched and rolled, great packets of water crashed down over the stern. When he went out on deck to check the rigging, he could hardly believe his eyes: sheltering from the wind was a sea swallow with a brass band. The bird recognized him and nestled into a fold of his oilskin. After the storm passed and clear sunlight bathed the sea, the bird rested with him for a long time. Then, not far from the Antarctic ice pack, it flew away. He never saw it again. But he would never forget that bird. The mystery of that meeting, of their two destinies twice crossing paths, will always remain unfathomable.

The old man blows out a mouthful of smoke. The sea swallows will not arrive today, he thinks. He will return tomorrow and sit on the same rock gazing out to sea, sure of the regularity of nature's calendar. For a few days every spring, the birds pass the headland beyond his village on their way back to the lagoon at the foot of the glacier. Not for anything in the world would he miss that sight.

Breeding

Wintering

Torpedo Birds
King Penguins

The South Pole is a world apart, an inaccessible fortress guarded by monstrous waves. Endlessly battered by howling winds and clouds of foam from the wave crests, it is a world that writes its own cruel rules. A few dark, rocky masses jut from the sea—barren, inhospitable islands etched by the swell, eternally shrouded in fog, on whose ragged shores enormous breakers deafeningly churn over gleaming stones and whose meager grass is forever flattened by wind.

As king penguins return from fishing, they frolic in the surf and jump onto the beach. For several days they have been swimming like torpedoes, following shoals of fish. Having eaten their fill, they waddle along in single file, clumsily making their way up the dune of rocks thrown up by the sea. Beyond, thousands of king penguins huddle together. The small fishing party hurries toward them, stumbling, spreading their fins to balance, eager to rejoin their mates.

Despite the sound of the waves and the wailing of the wind, each penguin instantly recognizes its companion's loud calls. Couples reunite, singing in unison, then gently rubbing beaks and caressing each other with their fins. Stooping, the male, who has remained on land, raises a fold of his belly to show off the white egg balanced on his large webbed feet. Then, with great care, the female huddles up to him and he gently rolls the egg onto her feet. It's her turn now to incubate their only egg while the father goes out to sea to eat. They will work in shifts to incubate and then rear the chick for nearly a year until it is able to fend for itself.

Many years ago, men as tough as the sea crossed the planet to brutally pillage the only riches of these tiny islands: king penguins. Every part of the birds was used by the hunters: the skin, the meat, and especially the fat, which was made into expensive oil. Every year people would return to club penguins to death and then plunge them in boiling water. The massacre went on for almost two centuries.

Luckily, those barbaric days are over. Vestiges of huts remain, despite the elements' dogged attempts to wipe out every trace of humans. Today, penguins have regained dominion over these far-flung specks of rock. Together they sing—through the storms and the scorning wind, through the rain and cold.

Height: 37 inches
Weight: 20–33 pounds
Fin length: 12–14 inches
Swimming speed: 7¹/₂ mph

The king penguin, like all penguins, cannot fly. On the other hand, it is perfectly adapted to its aquatic existence and is an excellent swimmer. In search of prey, it dives to depths of well over 500 feet, remaining underwater five minutes on average.

The king penguin eats mainly fish and squid, which it hunts underwater, on fishing trips lasting several days.

Penguins don't build a nest and they lay only one egg. The egg is incubated by the female for the first two days then by the male for the next six to twenty-one days, during which time he fasts.

At forty days old, the young form small day nurseries of three or four chicks each. Their parents leave separately on fishing trips. When they return, they recognize and locate their chick by its calls.

GREENLAND

NORTH AMERICA

BREEDING

WINTERING

Fliers in Formation
Snow Geese

Fall has decked the forests of northern Canada in its most beautiful shades. With a last sigh the magnificent trees turn red. In these lands where nature still reigns supreme, summer is having one last fling, an Indian summer in all its grandeur. Like an orchestra conductor, fall leads the leaves in a fiery crescendo before the symphony of winter begins.

A flock of birds flies in formation in the distance. It is a family of snow geese, their crisp, white plumage standing out against the forest's many hues. Forging ahead with rapid wing beats, fleeing the far north in a determined straight line, the parents know the elements unleashed by the oncoming cold are right at their heels. Many of them have already perished, caught up by the titanic forces invading the sky that swallow up the day with dark dense clouds, unleash hail and freezing rain, hurl down bolts of deadly lightning. Farther north, on the Arctic tundra closest to the North Pole, where the snow geese go each summer to breed, the wind's steely claws have already swept away their nests, the snow is covering over the lichens and mosses, and the ice is tightening its grip on the rivers and lakes. The ice cap is thickening, moving south almost visibly, snuffing out any life daring to resist it.

The parents lead the way, at the prow of the V. Their cutting through the air makes it easier for the young to follow. The young geese still have a carefree look in their eyes. Their parents must constantly watch over them for one wrong move. On this, their first migration, the young geese fly wide eyed, resenting having to learn the way and memorize every landmark they quickly pass over. But they will have to remember these places for when they later make the journey with a family of their own.

The many lakes dotted throughout this vast golden forest reflect the passing travelers, their all-white bodies and black wingtips fleetingly etched in the waters below, where, ahead of them, a camouflaged man wades carefully through the reeds, disturbing the mirrorlike surface and breaking the dialogue between earth and sky. His eyes follow the passing birds. A shot rings out, and a hail of buckshot crosses the geese's course. Flying faster, the parents encourage their young, exchanging brief looks— once again they have flown into the jaws of death and will hopefully fly out again.

Another shot hits one of the geese, and it plummets into the forest below. Flying as fast as she can, the mother goose watches her mate fall to earth. She knows that as far as the eye can see there will be no refuge. One of the cardinal rules of these winged wanderers is to never turn back. She will have to press on, leading her young to a safe haven. She will have to leave behind her loved one, the lively, protective fellow traveler she chose for life. The young follow their mother, who has fallen silent. They look back one last time toward the spot where their father fell, at the forest where gunfire struck him down. They will never forget.

People say that birds don't cry, but that's up to you to decide. Listen to what the wind whispers in your ear after the sun finishes its daily journey west. The wind will tell you that she dries the tears of these creatures, high in the sky, during the long migrations that often take them to a rendezvous with death, so often at the hands of humans.

Height: 25–31 inches
Weight: 5½–7¾ pounds
Wingspan: 50–64 inches
Flight speed: 34–59 mph

The adult snow goose is all white except for its black wing tips. Its pink beak has denticles (small toothlike projections) that enable it to rip out and grind the tubers and roots of aquatic plants growing around the water's edge. Its head plumage is sometimes tinted a rusty brown hue by iron deposits in the mud it feeds from.

In summer, it nests on the ground in the middle of the Arctic tundra. The chicks hatch in July and very soon leave the nest to feed on grass shoots. During this period, the parents molt completely and cannot fly for about three weeks, so the flock sets off on foot in search of food and an aquatic haven safe from predators such as arctic foxes.

Angels of the Seas

Great Albatrosses

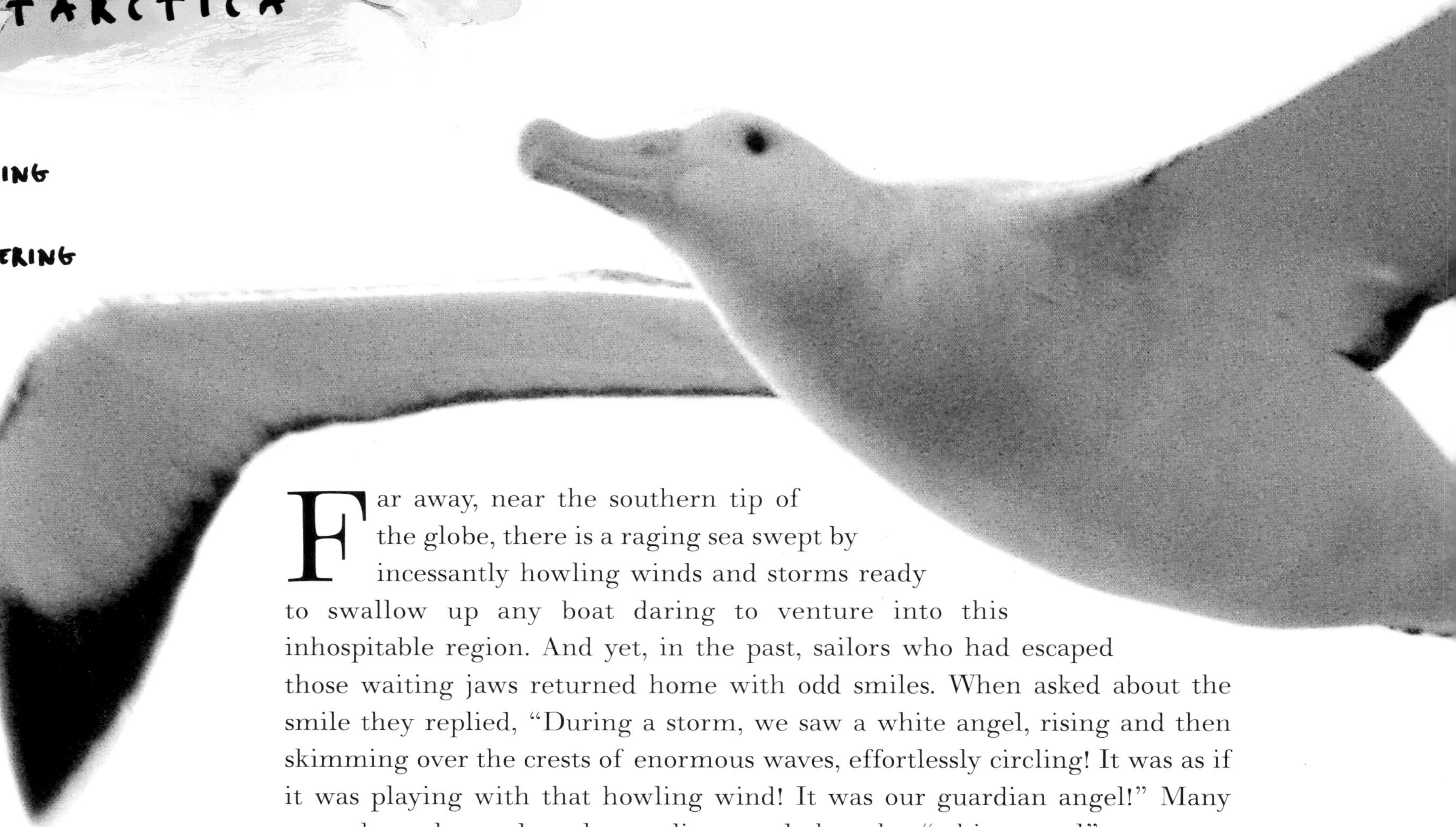

ANTARCTICA

Breeding

Wintering

F ar away, near the southern tip of the globe, there is a raging sea swept by incessantly howling winds and storms ready to swallow up any boat daring to venture into this inhospitable region. And yet, in the past, sailors who had escaped those waiting jaws returned home with odd smiles. When asked about the smile they replied, "During a storm, we saw a white angel, rising and then skimming over the crests of enormous waves, effortlessly circling! It was as if it was playing with that howling wind! It was our guardian angel!" Many years later, learned explorers discovered that the "white angel" was none other than a bird with light plumage and long wings. They called it the "great albatross" or "wandering albatross."

"For a long time I was a mystery to those creatures down below who watched me, mesmerized by my serene flight in the eye of the storm. I am the symbol of these cold, faraway southern seas. I glide with my wings fully spread—each of them over four feet long. The wind and sea are my allies. The wind is indispensable to me for taking off and flying, because of my body weight.

"I have been roaming the ocean waves alone for eight years now. I remember the tiny island lost in this raging sea where I was born, where not a single tree

24

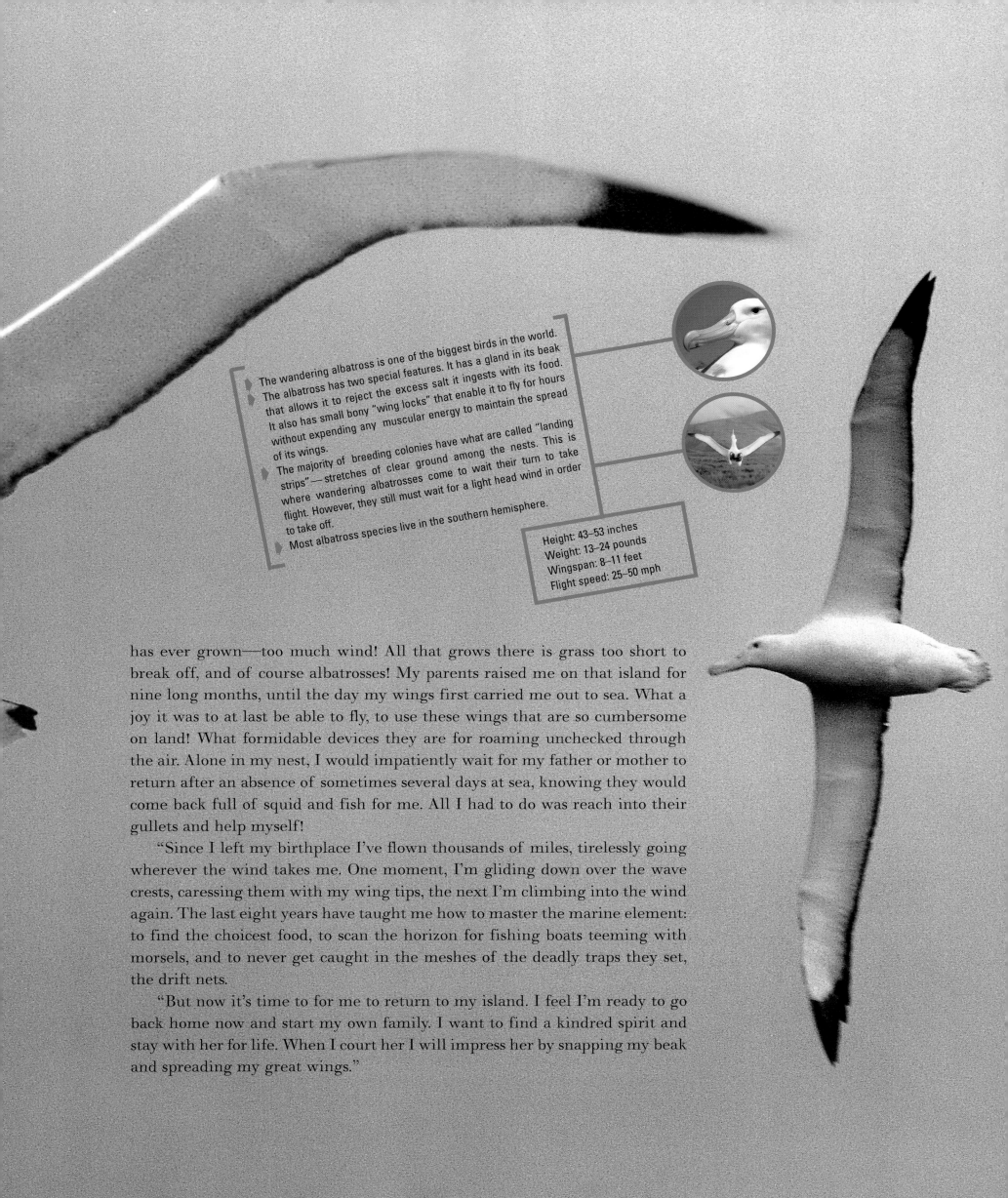

The wandering albatross is one of the biggest birds in the world.
The albatross has two special features. It has a gland in its beak that allows it to reject the excess salt it ingests with its food. It also has small bony "wing locks" that enable it to fly for hours without expending any muscular energy to maintain the spread of its wings.

The majority of breeding colonies have what are called "landing strips"—stretches of clear ground among the nests. This is where wandering albatrosses come to wait their turn to take flight. However, they still must wait for a light head wind in order to take off.

Most albatross species live in the southern hemisphere.

Height: 43–53 inches
Weight: 13–24 pounds
Wingspan: 8–11 feet
Flight speed: 25–50 mph

has ever grown—too much wind! All that grows there is grass too short to break off, and of course albatrosses! My parents raised me on that island for nine long months, until the day my wings first carried me out to sea. What a joy it was to at last be able to fly, to use these wings that are so cumbersome on land! What formidable devices they are for roaming unchecked through the air. Alone in my nest, I would impatiently wait for my father or mother to return after an absence of sometimes several days at sea, knowing they would come back full of squid and fish for me. All I had to do was reach into their gullets and help myself!

"Since I left my birthplace I've flown thousands of miles, tirelessly going wherever the wind takes me. One moment, I'm gliding down over the wave crests, caressing them with my wing tips, the next I'm climbing into the wind again. The last eight years have taught me how to master the marine element: to find the choicest food, to scan the horizon for fishing boats teeming with morsels, and to never get caught in the meshes of the deadly traps they set, the drift nets.

"But now it's time to for me to return to my island. I feel I'm ready to go back home now and start my own family. I want to find a kindred spirit and stay with her for life. When I court her I will impress her by snapping my beak and spreading my great wings."

White-Collared Acrobats
Mallards

BREEDING

WINTERING

PRESENT YEAR-ROUND

Height: 20–26 inches
Weight: 1½–3 pounds
Wingspan: 31–39 inches
Flight speed: 37–62 mph

▶ The mallard is one of the largest and most common European ducks. The male, with its bottle-green head and deep red breast, the green and red separated by a white band around the neck, is the most familiar. Mallards usually fly straight and fast but sometimes perform impressive aerobatics.

▶ The mallard is a "surface" duck since it doesn't dive for food but ducks its head underwater to graze on aquatic plants and poke around in the mud for small invertebrates. It also eats grass.

▶ Couples go into isolation to breed. The female lays between nine and thirteen eggs. Chicks are born covered with brown down, eyes open, and ready to follow their parents walking and swimming. They feed on their own, protected by their mother and sometimes their father. They can fly at two months.

A long time ago, monks cleared a wild region covered with thick forest. At the bottom of a small valley, they dug a pond to capture water from a tiny stream. Deep in the forest, pure water flowed from a spring up through mossy rocks. The monks' small dam provided them with water, fish during Lent, and power to turn the great wheel of their mill. The valley, until then so dark, now abounded with the new plants and animals that had arrived in the monks' wake to graze on the lush fields and inhabit the hedges and ponds they created.

A few centuries later, the pond became a marsh, a kingdom of birds. One morning as the spring sun, veiled by thin mist, bathed the water in pale yellow light, as the frogs and birds sang among the water lilies and reeds, a young boy from the city slipped down beneath the willows to the water's edge. Sitting motionless in the cool shade, he saw that a flock of mallards was living there. He decided to come watch them every day, hidden in the undergrowth. And as the weeks went by, the fierce mallards finally accepted his presence.

He never tired of admiring their iridescent plumage. In the calm of evening, he would gaze at the hypnotic shadows created in their wake, and delight at the sound of their wings when they sped overhead.

Soon there were baby ducklings, which would dive to the bottom to the pond and bob up again like corks. Sometimes one of them would go missing,

snapped up during the night by a polecat or pike. But life went on.

One morning the ducklings began trying to fly, and the little boy looked on in wonder and excitement, unconsciously jerking his shoulders up and down as if to encourage them.

One day, as a squadron of young mallards was flying around the valley in a wide circle, a black dot appeared from nowhere, closing in on them at lightning speed. It was a peregrine falcon, designed for speed, a bird that rarely misses its prey. But the prey's survival instinct is as strong as the hunter's. The ducks, hearing the barely perceptible sound of the bird of prey's sickle-shaped wings slicing through the air, made off in all directions and spiraled down toward the ground. The falcon, disoriented, missed its target. Quickly, it regained altitude for a second attempt, but the ducks had already disappeared. The attack lasted only a few seconds, during which the little boy held his breath, his heart racing. He understood that ducks learn to survive through chance encounters and perils like this.

Then fall came, a cool wind bending the reeds and plucking yellow leaves from the willows. The ducks flew south, heading toward the countless adventures their great journey held in store. The little boy returned to the city. He threw pieces of bread to the city ducks, who squabbled over them and jostled to peck food out of his hand. Those ducks were the spitting image of their country cousins—yet they were so tame! They were so big and fat that they no longer had the strength to fly. Sometimes their wings were even clipped, to render them even more docile. No thrilling aerobatics above reedy marshes for them, nor would they ever experience the joys and hardships of migration. He stood there lost in thought, a host of questions milling around in his brain. Since his stay on the banks of the marsh, he saw the fat ducks that paddled about in the murky city ponds, begging for stale crusts to the joy of the kids, in an entirely different light.

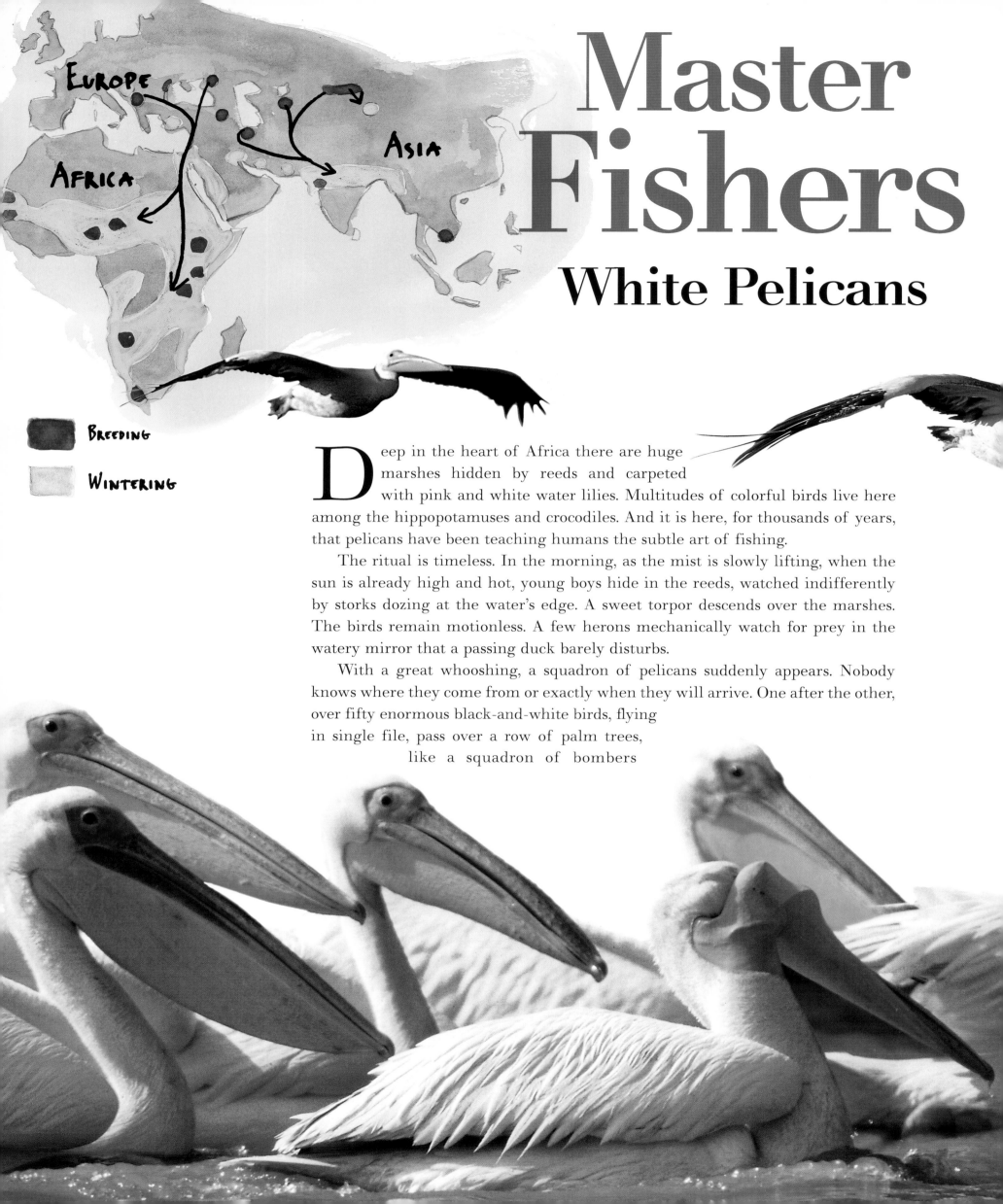

EUROPE

ASIA

AFRICA

■ BREEDING

□ WINTERING

Master Fishers
White Pelicans

Deep in the heart of Africa there are huge marshes hidden by reeds and carpeted with pink and white water lilies. Multitudes of colorful birds live here among the hippopotamuses and crocodiles. And it is here, for thousands of years, that pelicans have been teaching humans the subtle art of fishing.

The ritual is timeless. In the morning, as the mist is slowly lifting, when the sun is already high and hot, young boys hide in the reeds, watched indifferently by storks dozing at the water's edge. A sweet torpor descends over the marshes. The birds remain motionless. A few herons mechanically watch for prey in the watery mirror that a passing duck barely disturbs.

With a great whooshing, a squadron of pelicans suddenly appears. Nobody knows where they come from or exactly when they will arrive. One after the other, over fifty enormous black-and-white birds, flying in single file, pass over a row of palm trees, like a squadron of bombers hedgehopping as they approach their target, gliding silently without ruffling a single feather. One final turn and they land on the marsh, feet out in front, with a splash.

The pelicans are here to fish. They ignore the young spies hidden in the reeds. Herons, egrets, storks, ducks, cormorants—all the marsh birds make way for the invading party. As soon as they arrive they begin stretching their legs and the huge skin pouch that hangs beneath their beak by craning their head in every direction. After a short rest, they form an evenly spaced rank and start swimming toward the opposite bank, beating the water with their beaks and wings. Little by little, the rank moves into a semicircle, driving hundreds of fish toward a shallow dead end.

The semicircle gradually closes, trapping the fish inside. Then, as if signaled, the pelicans plunge their long fishnet-shaped beaks into the water in unison. Some of them use their feet and wings to reach deeper, some disappear underwater completely. Everywhere, fish are jumping out of the water to escape their voracious beaks. In the ensuing splashing, wing-thrashing free-for-all, the groaning pelicans fight fiercely over the choicest morsels.

Finally each bird draws back, satisfied, its pouch full. Some have caught catfishes so enormous they have deformed and ripped the beak pouch with their spines. The fishing is over. The young boys, perfectly still, look on in wonder.

The pelicans are sated. After shaking themselves one more time in the warm water, one after the other they run across the water, then haul themselves ponderously into the air. With a few slow, powerful wing beats, they find a pocket of hot air and glide effortlessly upward. They become white dots against the blue sky, and then they vanish.

Calm descends over the marsh. Multicolored birds are already going about their business. The boys make their way back to the village, impatient to one day become master fishers too.

Height: 58–70 inches
Weight: 11–33 pounds
Wingspan: 8–11½ feet
Flight speed: 19–37 mph

▶ The white pelican is one of the largest and heaviest birds.
▶ Pelicans are highly social creatures, always flying, fishing, and nesting together.
▶ Very timid, they build their nests in locations inaccessible to terrestrial predators, often on sandbanks or in the middle of lakes and rivers. The female lays one or two eggs, which both parents take turns to sit on. The chicks hatch one after the other, featherless. Their pink skin quickly goes black, and a brown down begins to grow at around two weeks. At twenty to twenty-five days old, the young pelicans begin to leave their nests to form day nurseries of sometimes more than 100 birds.
▶ White pelicans can fly at 65 to 70 days old, when they become completely independent. They reach sexual maturity at three to four years.

Sea
Daggers
Gannets

North America

Atlantic Ocean

Europe

Africa

Breeding

Wintering

Off the coast of Scotland is a remote island where nothing grows, for only rocks can withstand the endless waves. It is called Bass Rock.

"I don't know what made me do it—it may have been my parent's eyes, lined with blue, reflecting the sea stretching away to the horizon. Or was it the incessant breeze that ruffled my brand-new feathers, caressing my face, beckoning me? That famous breeze that rose from the foot of the cliffs and already filled me with longing when my body was still only covered with down, whispering wonderful tales in my ears …

"Suddenly I spread my wings and like a feather I was swept away by the wind! Nothing could stop me. There was no going back. In that moment, I forged my lifelong bond with that invisible force that comes from nowhere yet is so perceptible, so sensitive to every slightest movement of my feathers. A pact had been sealed with it forever. It would support me during my every flight and protect me from storms by sending me advance warning of their location. So be it. Let this force carry me far south when the time comes, when the cold tightens its grip on my island birthplace.

"I'm rising very quickly over the colony. Everything's so easy up here; playing with the air is a real pleasure. Young birds, still in their nests, watch

Height: 35–37 inches
Weight: 5–8 pounds
Wingspan: 64–70 inches
Flight speed: 62 mph

▶ The gannet's plumage is solid white with black markings on its wing tips. Its head turns a buff color during the mating season in spring. It uses its long, narrow wings to glide like the albatross does in the southern hemisphere, descending low over the waves, then turning into the wind to quickly regain altitude.

▶ The gannet has a gland on its beak to reject the excess salt it ingests, and an oil-secreting gland in each eye to protect its cornea from salt.

▶ The gannet's binocular vision enables it to judge distances extremely accurately, and so optimize its chances of catching fish, which it hones in on from around thirty feet up before launching into one of its lightning dives.

with longing to take to the sky. Their parents, sure they're not ready yet, dissuade them. They know there's no room for mistakes on your maiden flight. At the top of that sheer cliff, one slip and you'll plummet to the sea below, where the waves will swallow you and spit you out onto the rocks. The sky is a deep blue, the island is just a tiny dot now in the infinite ocean. I am going fishing with the adults for the first time. When we locate shoals in the vicinity, we will perform those famous high dives that never cease to amaze wingless creatures.

"For my first dive, nothing will matter except getting my beak around a fish startled by my sudden intrusion into its realm. From up on high, their metallic reflections form a silver river whose sparkle is our signal to plunge down into the watery world below. For a few moments I will leave the breeze behind me, wings folded, slicing down like a dagger through the air. Fleeing fish will splash through the waves crossing our path. With beaks like sharp magnets, drawn magically to them, we will gorge ourselves. But the sea, furious at our piracy, will soon repel us. Like the air bubbles that don't mix with the dark-eyed water, we will regain the surface, our fish already swallowed. And, Breeze, we'll be yours again! Our pact rekindled in an instant, an updraft effortlessly plucking us up and away into the sky, where my long journey south awaits me. Where all the wonderful stories the breeze has been whispering in my ears will at last come true."

SIBERIA

JAPAN

EUROPE

ASIA

Snowbirds
Whooper Swans

■ REPRODUCTION

□ WINTERING

In Japan, the Land of the Rising Sun, white birds are said to carry snowflakes from faraway Siberia in their plumage. This is why the Japanese call whooper swans "snowbirds." Whenever farmers see these birds flying in groups, they say they suddenly feel a cool breeze, which sends a little shiver through them. The birds' passage signals the continuation of the ancestral cycle of the seasons. They know that soon glacial cold will descend on them, enveloping them in its infinite ice crystals, and that their familiar surroundings will be rapidly cloaked in a mantle of snow sprinkled from the sky.

The days draw in, crops cease to grow, chimneys begin to smoke in the valleys, nature gradually shrivels up, and winter sets in. The snowbirds have returned, gracing Japan with their presence and heralding radiant, crystal-clear winter days.

The snowflakes have stopped falling. The first rays of the sun pierce smoke rising from a distant volcano. Thick snow everywhere deadens all sound. The trees, every branch and twig coated with ice, sparkle in the morning sun. During the night small piles of snow have appeared on the frozen lake, a sacred lake where hot springs melt holes in the ice, where the swans come and land in the evening, disappearing in the rising steam. It is said that the birds turn into snow during the night and are reborn in the morning with brand-new white feathers, the winter tirelessly clothing them in its most beautiful and purest color.

It is in the first glow of the coming day that one begins to hear muffled calls coming from the steam that rises from the lake, from the many piles of snow lit now by the sun. A head and then a long neck emerges from one of them. A snowbird waking up! The swan repeats its call, louder this time. One by one, like successive